BEYOND

LECTOR HOUSE PUBLIC DOMAIN WORKS

BEYOND

HENRY SEWARD HUBBARD

ISBN: 978-93-5420-660-3

Published: 1896

LECTOR HOUSE LLP
E-MAIL: lectorpublishing@gmail.com

BEYOND

BY

HENRY SEWARD HUBBARD

1896

TO
LOVERS OF THE TRUTH,
WHATEVER
LAND MAY CLAIM THEM FOR ITS OWN,
TO THE
EARNEST MEN AND WOMEN
OF MY TIME,
THIS BOOK IS RESPECTFULLY
DEDICATED.

PREFACE.

A word of explanation in reference to my title may be appropriately given here. By Beyond, I mean what is sometimes called the unseen world, but which might better be called the immaterial world, since that which distinguishes it from the world proper is not merely that it is invisible, but that it cannot be made visible to mortal eyes.

However, I have not assumed to treat of all that the word might be made to cover, but have confined myself mostly to that territory, with the entrance to it, which may be said to adjoin the earth, and which therefore is more immediately interesting and important to be acquainted with, and have addressed myself especially to those who seem to be constitutionally unable to perceive the reality of this other world, although willing and anxious to be convinced.

If there is any one thing more than another which I hope to convey, it is that the truths which pertain to the superior life do not conflict with common sense, however they may rise beyond the perfect grasp of that power of the mind.

HENRY SEWARD HUBBARD.

CONTENTS

Page

1. CHAPTER I.. 1

2. CHAPTER II.. 3

3. CHAPTER III.. 5

4. CHAPTER IV.. 7

5. CHAPTER V.. 9

6. CHAPTER VI.. 11

7. CHAPTER VII.. 13

8. CHAPTER VIII.. 14

9. CHAPTER IX.. 15

10. CHAPTER X.. 18

11. CHAPTER XI.. 19

12. CHAPTER XII.. 21

13. CHAPTER XIII.. 23

14. CHAPTER XIV.. 25

15. CHAPTER XV.. 28

16. CHAPTER XVI.. 31

17. CHAPTER XVII.. 34

18. CHAPTER XVIII.. 36

19. CHAPTER XIX.. 38

20. CHAPTER XX.. 40

21. CHAPTER XXI. 42

22. CHAPTER XXII. 44

23. CHAPTER XXIII. 46

24. CHAPTER XXIV. 47

25. CHAPTER XXV. 48

26. CHAPTER XXVI. 51

27. CHAPTER XXVII. 53

INTRODUCTION.

TO MY BROTHERS AND SISTERS, GREETING.

I had known for some time that I had a book to write, but not exactly how I was going to set about it, when there fell under my notice the following appeal, whose unique and touching eloquence, I venture to say, is without a parallel in our literature.

"There have always been those, and now they are more numerous than ever, who maintain that the dead do return.

"Far be it from me to dogmatically negative the assertions of honest, earnest men engaged in the study of a subject so awful, so reverent, so solemn, where the student stands with a foot on each side of the boundary-line between two worlds.

"We know a little of the hither, can we know aught of the thither world?" 'How pure in heart, how sound in head, with what affections bold,' should be the explorer on a voyage so sublime! Never from 'peak of Darien' did the flag of exploration fly over the opening up of a realm so mighty.

"How stale and trite the fleet of a Magellan to the adventurous soul who would circumnavigate the archipelagoes of the dead!"

"How commonplace Pizarro to him who would launch forth on that black and trackless Pacific across the expanse of which has ever lain the dread and the hope of our race!"

"They know little who are robed in university gowns. What know they who are robed in shrouds? We gather but little from the platform; what can we learn from the grave? The wisdom of the press is foolishness. Is there no voice from the sepulchre? It is we, not you, who are in darkness, O ye dead! The splendor of the iris of eternity has flashed on your plane of vision; but our heavy eyelids droop in the shadow of the nimbus of time.

"Can you tell us naught? Can we never know your secret till, in the dust, we lay down our bones with yours?"

"We are here in the care, the poverty, the sin, and, above all, in the darkness. Oh, if ye can, have mercy on us; shed a ray from your shekinah-light athwart the darkness of our desolation. We are trodden down by our brothers among the living. Help us, our fathers from the dead."[1]

---

[1] Editor *The Agnostic Journal*, London, England.

How profoundly these words moved me cannot easily be told, for my entire life, up to this point, seems to have been made up of the various stages of a preparation enabling me to respond to just such an appeal as this, echoed, as I know full well it is, from the hearts of thousands of my fellow-beings. Yet one who should enter the rose-embowered cottage by the sea where I sit writing, would never dream that I guard treasures of knowledge gathered in the hidden realm that lies beyond the sense.

For years have passed, and lonely life has changed to family life, and there have been times when I have felt almost at home again within the confines of the purely earthly realm of thoughts and things. Not quite, however, for that would be impossible. And now, shall I branch out in a tale of strange adventure? Shall I seek to convey to my readers what led to those experiences which have so isolated me in thought? Shall I describe their outward aspect, the channel through which they were received, as for instance, a dream, a trance, a vision, or *other ways less known*?

To do so might amuse or entertain, but that is not my object. Besides, I understand thoroughly that in these modern days it is the truth, and not the truth-teller, that is wanted. If a man has anything to say, let him say it, and if it bear the stamp of truth, if it will stand the test of analysis the most severe, it will be accepted. If not, he may show a ticket of his travels beyond the moon, but that will not avail him.

All that I ask of my readers is that they will permit me to write of that realm which is so hidden from mortals that many of them deny its very existence, as though I knew all about it. Whether I do or not, no mere statement, in the absence of other evidence, could in the least decide.

THE AUTHOR.

BEYOND.

CHAPTER I.

In the world of thought to-day, few things are more significant than the extent to which the religious dogmas of the past are being questioned, analyzed, and, in general, made to give account of themselves.

People are discovering that it is lawful to use the mind as a crucible, and to submit any and all statements, irrespective of their age, to the electric current of modern fearlessness of thought, before accepting them as truth.

Scientific formulas, many of them, fare little better, and are made to yield up the kernel of fact they contain, stripped of the husk of theory in which it has long been buried.

For the living truth is demanded such value as we obtain in our own life-experiences, if possible; and whenever this can be obtained without paying the price it costs us in life, of pain, or loss, or a mortgaged future, then, indeed, the demand becomes imperious.

And this has become especially true of late years in regard to things occult. Formerly the boundaries of the earth-life marked the limit of thought and aspiration, and those who seemed to have the widest experience within those bounds were often the loudest in proclaiming their utter failure to find any lasting satisfaction in all that life could give. Vanity of vanities, all is vanity, was echoed and re-echoed until the gloomy thought spread like a cloud over the sky, chilling all noble effort, and blighting the aspirations of the young and hopeful. But a brighter day has dawned. These boundaries, which formerly seemed like walls impenetrable, have grown thin and shadowy, and it is astonishing to note how people everywhere are asking, as with open mind, Is this future life we have heard of so long, an actual fact? If so, what is the nature of it? What are its relations to present facts? and how may I obtain a common-sense view of it? Just what are its relations to me, and what are mine to a future life? Where can I obtain clear light on the subject?

This condition of things brings it to pass that a peculiar responsibility rests upon one, like the writer, to whom has been given extraordinary facilities for acquiring the knowledge now so greatly in demand. To relate what those facilities were, how or why given, and what price in the currency of the hidden realm was paid for so much of its treasures as was brought away, might interest the curious, as I have suggested, but it would not materially affect the value of what is to be given. That must stand or fall by its intrinsic worth, not by the circumstances associated with its acquirement.

It may be imparted, however, that this knowledge was obtained at a period separated from the present by an interval of fourteen years, that so momentous were the personal experiences associated therewith, that the few weeks during which they occurred, together with those immediately preceding and following, seem to constitute, as it were, a separate existence, whose length, if it were to be measured by such events as leave their indelible impress on the soul, far exceeds the entire remainder of my life.

That I have kept this knowledge locked up so long has been due to various causes beyond my control, and I am more than glad that I am at last able to put on record some fragments of it, at least, whose value I do not underestimate, although very rarely in the history of the world has it been given out in this way.

CHAPTER II.

Perhaps I cannot open my subject in any better way than by giving a few reasons why a knowledge of The Beyond has remained a sealed book for centuries.

My first reason will not be a very satisfactory one, because I cannot now enter into it as fully as I could wish; but it belongs first, and cannot be omitted. A knowledge of The Beyond has remained hidden from men, first, because those intelligences who were capable of imparting it have refrained from doing so. Some of these intelligences were actuated by selfish motives. They could more easily control those whom they hoped to enslave, by keeping them ignorant. Others have remained silent out of respect for an edict proceeding from a far height at a time when all men were believers in a future state, and so many of them were absorbed in speculating upon it, and holding communications with the departed, that the earth was neglected, and in danger of going to waste. Hence the edict, which was promulgated through the kings who were able themselves to see the need of it.

Another very important reason why this knowledge has remained hidden, is because to embody it in a language appropriate to it, and, at the same time, avoid obscurity, is exceedingly difficult.

Why? Because it belongs to a different world, a world which has no nearer relation to this one than thoughts have to things. To illustrate what I mean by this, suppose you should wake up some night and find yourself in silent darkness and unable to move a muscle. Suppose you could not even feel the bed under you, being conscious only of being supported in a horizontal position. So long as these avenues of sense remained closed, the world of things would not exist to you, and you could not say, of your own knowledge, that it continued to exist for anyone else.

While the situation would be a startling one without doubt, I am going to assume that you would have a sufficient degree of self-control to keep your mental balance. This would be the easier as you discovered that your mental vision was as clear as ever, and that your real self, which is back of all your senses, had received no shock or injury. You would naturally wish to know just what had happened, and it would be apt to disturb you somewhat to find that your reasoning powers failed to respond when you called upon them to solve the problem, as naturally they would, since the brain, with which they do their work, would share the inaction of the body. Now, if the world of things had thus vanished, what could remain? In the first place, memory. You would be able to call up the pictures of the past, and live over again in your mind any scene there depicted. But you would not be confined to living in the past. Although unable to see or to hear, you would be able to assume the mental attitude either of looking or listening, and as you sought to penetrate the gloom of your surroundings, you would be conscious of lifting eyelids which perhaps had never been raised before, and the mystic light of another world would dawn upon you. Shadowy forms of graceful outline would be seen, at first dimly, then with greater clearness. You would not mistake them for mortals, and, having no acquaintance with other-world intelligences, you might take them for moving pictures, destitute of any kind of life.

Presently you would become aware that connected thoughts were passing through your mind, without conscious volition on your part, and assuming the attitude of a listener you would discover that the inner world of sound was opening to you. The subject treated of might not relate to you personally, but you would hail with delight the opportunity to prove yourself in communication with other minds.

Presently some sentiment is expressed which you do not approve, and you put forth an impulse of will-power in protest. Instantly comes a thought-message directly to you. Who has arrested my current of thought? The meaning of this is at once apparent. You are like a telegraph operator who has been listening to a passing message, containing a false statement, and has stopped it. You might now withdraw your protest and allow the message to pass as something which did not concern you, or you might assert your individuality and reply to the sharp question by saying, "Because I allow nothing to pass through my mind which I do not approve." If you adopted the first course, you might be let off with a curse, and told to mind your own business hereafter; but if you should manifest the temerity indicated by the second, a thundering "What?" might fall upon your new sense, and you would discover that you had a fight on your hands. It may be supposed that you would mentally assume an upright position, which in that world corresponds to the act of rising here, and brace yourself for the contest. But it is not necessary to carry the illustration any farther at this time. I merely wished to show how *thoughts* may take the place of *things* in the mind's arena when, for any reason, things are shut out.

A third reason why a knowledge of The Beyond is not more generally disseminated, is that false ideas in regard to death are so predominant that it has become a habit with the great majority to dismiss from the mind all thoughts having, or that are supposed to have, any possible connection with it, and therefore the avenue of approach to the minds of such is kept closed by themselves.

It may be asked why the solitary student is not able to attain to a satisfactory solution of the great problem, although seeking it with utmost earnestness. And I answer, first, because he probably seeks for it in the same way that he would seek for earth-knowledge, which is an error; and, secondly, because those who would otherwise gladly give it to him are able to read his motives, and finding them purely selfish, they turn away and leave him, while those spirits who have occult knowledge to *sell*, demand pay in a coin which the student is seldom willing to give, namely, a certain degree of control over him.

CHAPTER III.

Mathematicians have frequently discussed the possibility of what is called a fourth dimension.

They have shown by clear reasoning that if we could suppose a person to be acquainted only with objects of two dimensions, that is, plane surfaces, the possibility of a third would be as difficult to comprehend as now are the speculations on a possible fourth. For instance, it would be as mysterious an operation to transfer anything from one point to another without moving it along the surface that lay between, as is now the manipulation of solid objects, like the passage of matter through matter, by the masters of occult science.

This fine example of reasoning from the known to the unknown may be compared to Leverrier's researches in one respect, and that the most important one, namely, that the looked-for fact in all verity awaits discovery, and that the scientist who shall first boldly declare that the objective world about us, which seems to occupy and does occupy all of space that we can reach by ordinary means of thought, is merely a veil which hides a world just as real, and having just as real relations to us, as the first is supposed to monopolize, and which, in its essential nature, is independent of space, and its concomitant, time,—whoever, I say, shall first boldly declare this, will fairly win a crown of laurel.

When I say that this world has real relations to us, I do not mean us as mere aggregations of matter in a highly organized form; I mean us, the creatures of hope and fear, of joy and depression, gay at heart or careworn with responsibility; us to whom friendship, love, and purity are realities and not mere names, and who cherish the firm belief that loyalty to our ideals and devotion to truth are immortal in their nature, and that it may be possible that we ourselves may yet become as impassive to the assaults of time.

Shall I say us, also, the creatures of doubt and despair, whose sky is hopelessly clouded, and to whom anything resembling happiness has become only a memory? The world of which I speak has the same direct relations to us all.

The idea is a common one that this invisible world is to be sought, if at all, among the imponderable gases, that if it have objectivity, as it is supposed it must have, the nature of it will resemble these forms of matter; and that by traveling out in thought, so to speak, along this line, we shall presently arrive at a sufficiently accurate concept of what these invisible realities are like.

It is this delusion, that the unseen is by so much the unreal, instead of the contrary, that I hope to do something to destroy.

Let me give an example of occult power of a scientific sort, as exercised by free spirits.

One wishes to speak to a friend. What does he do? He simply speaks the name of that friend in his mind. Immediately, and without further effort on his part, there appears before his mental vision a clear outline representation of the form of that friend, ready to answer with perfect distinctness any question that may be asked of him. It is telephone communication without apparatus, and with the appearance of the friend. Were the two in close sympathy, perhaps engaged in the same kind of spiritual labor, so that the question would be of a kind not unexpected, the rapidity of action common to spirits would make it possible to ask the question and receive the answer in an infinitesimal fraction of a second.

I have called this occult power of a scientific sort. By this I mean to indicate, what is sometimes forgotten, that The Beyond has its science as well as religion, and that it is only because its science has been a sealed book so long and the corruption of revealed religion has been so great, that, as a result, the acceptance of occult science itself as truth is called, by some, *religion*, although removed from it as by infinity. It is true, however, that the devotee to occult science who shall persistently declare its genuineness in the face of opposition, scorn, or even persecution, is on the road to illumination, and he may himself become a gateway between physical life and death, through which may pass and repass the message, the tone, or even the phantom form which testifies of a world beyond the grave. To such a one, his belief becomes a sure and certain knowledge of a scientific fact, as verified by sympathetic experience times without number; and the time is not far distant when these attainments will receive the same recognition, as belonging to the domain of reality, as those of physical science now do.

CHAPTER IV.

Science, as such, is a knowledge of physical facts. Religion, as such, is an apprehension of spiritual truths.

The work of the scientist is to separate facts from delusions, and then to arrange and classify his knowledge. The work of the religionist is to separate truth from error, to make it effectual in practice, and give it to the world.

In their essence, science and religion are neither enemies nor friends. They are not necessarily associates, but their respective domains are included in the domain of thought, and thought is an attribute of the ego. The ego in us, then, is in touch with both religion and science: with science, primarily, through this material body, which, surcharged with vital magnetism, moves at its will; and with religion through that inner conscious self which so avoids expression through matter, that it may remain contentedly under lock for more than half a lifetime, and which, even when released, may need a special impulse to induce it to express itself in words.

The religious nature in man is, in fact, so hidden that it seems at times impossible to draw it out in any manifestation whatever, which fact causes many to deny its existence altogether; and there is to-day a widely prevalent doctrine, world-wide I might say among scholars, that all the facts observable which could possibly be grouped under the head of religion may readily be distributed among mere physical phenomena on the one hand, and scientific or intellectual on the other.

The skepticism in regard to the verbal authority of the sacred writings is intimately associated with the same doctrine, as is shown by the way the errors and the truth of the Bible are made to seem one, and the whole is rejected as error.

It is taught, in effect, that all which goes by the name of religion is unworthy the serious attention of the thoughtful, that it had its origin in the barbarous stage of our development as a race, and ought to be laid aside as a garment outgrown. The days of this particular form of unbelief are numbered.

Why? Because it is to be demonstrated that religion is something more than moonlight vaporings of the credulous, something other than the simple faith of children; that religion is not only a spiritual reality, but that it has a body of its own.

In order that the meaning of this statement may not be mistaken, let it be remembered that some of the most powerful forms of matter, electricity, for example, are entirely invisible.

Therefore, when I say that religion has a body of its own, it is not necessary to go delving for anything. That body itself may be undiscoverable by any sense save feeling. Have you ever been in the presence of a man who could fairly be said to *embody* religion? Of those who manifest its spirit so pure and unselfish, there are comparatively few in the world, but of those who, to that spirit, add a full manly or womanly strength, the number is brought so low that multitudes of people may perhaps never have come in contact with any. Such as these bear about with them a consciousness of power so great as to utterly destroy every kind of fear save one, the fear of doing wrong. The name of Savonarola will occur to many of my readers.

It ought not to be necessary to add that I am using the word religion in a different sense from that attaching to it in such a phrase as the World's Parliament of Religions.

If I should say, There are many sciences, yet science is one, I should expect to be fairly well understood.

I would make the parallel declaration, There are many religions, but religion is one.

CHAPTER V.

Is there any common ground on which science and religion meet? There is. They meet in modern Spiritualism.

But because modern Spiritualism consists of a body of facts and theories on the one hand, and a countless number of soul-stirring experiences on the other, it follows that it takes a great many different people to fairly represent modern Spiritualism.

Some have devoted themselves to it exclusively on the religious side, others as exclusively on the scientific side. According to the bent of their nature, and with an equal degree of courage, the earnest, devoted students of science, on the one hand, and those of religion, on the other, are approaching from opposite poles this forbidden ground.

Disregarding the warnings of the older religious teachers, that evil, and only evil, haunts the grewsome place, one wing of the army of truth-seekers is making the discovery that if all the manifestations of modern spiritualism are to be attributed to one source, and that an evil one, then never was a house so divided against itself before. They are prepared to show that some of its most astonishing phenomena begin and end in good to all who witness them, and they declare that only a culpable misuse of the powers of the mind would lead to any other inference than that these good results come originally from good sources, and are therefore worthy of that reverence which of right belongs to the good, wherever it appears.

The other wing of the army of truth-seekers also contains its heroes. Have you not told us, they say to the great scientists who have laid down the principles on which investigations of all kinds should be conducted, that science claims the world for its field, and especially the world of phenomena?

Why, then, do so many of our captains and colonels, who should represent the thought of the higher officers, so persistently endeavor to prevent us from obtaining for ourselves the store of facts upon which, we are told, the theories of spiritualism are based?

Is it possible for us to have intelligent opinions even, to say nothing of carefully-drawn conclusions on this matter, without following the usual course, so strenuously insisted on in all other branches of scientific research, that of personally observing the phenomena for ourselves? And so when they get no answer to this, or no answer which satisfies those who love the truth for its own sake, they proceed, these scientific explorers, and with caution enter the unknown country, avoiding, as far as possible, that portion which they recognize as especially occupied by the other division of truth-seekers before described.

And they find no lack of material upon which to exercise the keenest faculties of their minds, while their interest becomes so great that they are soon ready to exclaim, Why was I kept away from here so long?

All indications, say they, favor the idea that in this direction rather than in any other is to be sought the solution of that profoundest of mysteries, the problem of life, and, with faces aglow with interest, they pursue their explorations, always ready, however, to declare that they have not changed their course, they are still in the pursuit of science and have not the slightest idea of joining hands with religionists on any pretext whatever.

All of which goes to show that the realm of the occult may be conveniently divided into two grand divisions, one of which may be called occult science, and the other occult religion; and that part of both which has been recently brought to view is the domain known as modern Spiritualism, where, as I have said, science and religion meet. I wish it could be said that scientists, as such, and religious teachers, as such, have also not only met, but shaken hands across the narrow line which still divides them even here, on this which I have called a common ground.

But it is to be feared that there is all too little thought of any possible terms of peace between the opposing forces.

Let us hope that out from the cloudy mysteries of the debatable land itself may come the gleam of a star whose brightness shall illumine all who lift their eyes, and whose pure, sweet influence shall change foes to friends, as heart shall answer heart beneath its shining.

CHAPTER VI.

THERE are many, however, who have an invincible repugnance to this method of research, and I would here say for the benefit of such, that while I am on friendly terms with spiritualists generally, I am not indebted to them for what I have to give. My observations of the phenomena of spiritualism, although wide and varied, have all been made since I came to know, independently, that there are intelligences above man, and that there is a world distinctly different from this, where they have their home.

Spiritualistic phenomena, as observed through mediums, have, in a general way, confirmed what I knew in regard to the other world, but I find many of the prevalent ideas which are supposably based on these phenomena to be erroneous in the extreme. For instance, it is taught as a doctrine that there is no death, and those who teach it point triumphantly to the demonstrations of the survival of those whose mortal part has been laid in the grave, not realizing that in so doing they prove themselves to be still in bondage to the old error, that death and annihilation are one and the same, and that consequently whoever has escaped the one, must necessarily have escaped the other.

To prove that a man who has severed his connection with the mortal state has not suffered annihilation, proves nothing whatever as to his acquaintance with death.

Even the passing from one world to the other, which is commonly associated with death, is not the same thing, for many possess the power of so passing while still tenants of the clay.

If death, then, is not annihilation, nor the mere passing from one kind of life into another, what is it? It is the severing of the magnetic bonds which unite the body of the individual to the body of the race as a whole.

We do not often consider what an important element in our lives are these magnetic currents which link us to our fellows.

Silent and invisible as they are, they hold us with a tremendous power. What our friends, our neighbors, our relatives think us capable of doing, that we can do with comparative ease; but anything out of the common, calling for the exercise of ability which they do not suppose us to possess—how nearly impossible it is for us to do it, however conscious we may be of the inherent power!

As a part of the race we are bound to it by magnetic currents so long as our mortal life continues, and the cutting off of these currents by death may be to our consciousness the greatest misfortune or the greatest happiness we have ever known.

Now I am not preaching, I am simply stating that which I know to be true. I know it in the same way that I know anything wherein experience shuts out even the shadow of a doubt.

To speak of the misfortune of death: suppose you were a clock which for twenty-five years had been a part of the world's life, keeping good time and always on duty. Then suppose you were suddenly laid away in the dark and dusty attic of a warehouse until some estate should be settled that would require an indefinite number of years.

The comparison is not perfect. The clock is not only mostly automatic, as we are, but entirely so. That in our nature which is essentially free is not even touched by death, but the bodily activities and associations may be our only field of action, and these are cut off absolutely, while memory recalls every event of the life that is finished, and especially every decision which has had the slightest influence upon our destiny. The positive element in us which has found constant vent in physical action is rendered helpless by the complete paralysis of all the motor nerves. We cannot even think, for this requires some movement of the brain. A consciousness of being left behind while the world travels on, a feeling that this experience had not been foreseen in the least, nor in any way provided against, spite of warnings which now seem to echo and re-echo through the darkness — these are what is left us in place of the sunlight, the breezes of evening, the voices of children, the light of the stars.

But death may be release, it may be happiness, it may be ecstasy beyond the power of words to tell. We may have cast the long look ahead in time. We may have decided that since bodily life is limited at best, it shall not be first in our regards: its appetites, its demands, shall not take precedence above those calls which find their answer in the depths of being, calls to rise out of the mire of reckless self-indulgence, and clothe ourselves in the garb of a true manhood and womanhood, taking for our model those who count not their life dear unto them, but reach out for eternal values.

The pathway is not wide, and they who pursue it may find themselves at close of life (I am not speaking especially of old age) almost alone. The energies of the spirit have grown by constant exercise, and the soul has grown strong, imparting its vibrations to the body, which has so responded that, one after another, the magnetic links which have held it to the slower progress of the race have snapped asunder. We are far ahead, and the spirit longs for purer air than it can find on earth. We have anticipated all the pains of death. We have endured them in our struggle for the mastery of ourselves. Death now but sets the seal upon our victory, gives us the freedom we have earned, ushers us into the society for which we have prepared ourselves, crowns us heirs of immortality.

Now, whether death shall be this happiness or that misery, in either case it will be remembered as a great fact of consciousness, the greatest ever known, and the doctrine that there is no death will never be able to find lodgment in the minds of those who have experienced it.

CHAPTER VII.

It may be worth our while to inquire how this extremely modern doctrine came into being, and if we can solve the problem, it may reflect light upon the genesis of other doctrines very much older and equally erroneous.

There is something so startling, so unexpected, in the phrase, "There is no death," that we are quite safe in assuming that it did not originate in the mind of a mortal. In fact, one would be obliged first to disown his mortality before he could utter it with any consciousness of speaking the truth. If, then, the words have come from the Beyond, it would appear that some super-mundane intelligence has been promulgating error. But let us not be too hasty. Let us remember that in our grandfather's time the great majority of people looked upon death as the termination of existence. It was an impenetrable darkness. Those who claimed to know anything different were so few, and their evidence was so mysterious, as to have a scarcely perceptible effect on this portion of our race. Death had come to mean annihilation, and when the age-long dictum, shutting the two worlds apart, was removed, those spirit-teachers who were commissioned to scatter the darkness were obliged to use expedients. Laying aside their own understanding of the word death, and taking up the erroneous meaning attached to it by those whom they wished to reach, they sent out this incisive denial, There is no death. The paraphrase would be, There is no such death as you believe in, which was the truth, and had the effect of truth upon the minds of those who heard it, lifting them out of the darkness, flashing upon them, light. The word was a medicine of wonderful effect, but it was not intended as a food, and spiritualists of to-day who make it a part of their daily diet are most seriously injured thereby. Who that has ever attended the average séance but can recall the careless trifling, the insensate levity, of many while waiting for the hour. By their conduct they seem to say, What is death more than a mere journey to another country? Or a séance, what is it more than a telephone office? Most startling will be the event to such as these.

CHAPTER VIII.

BUT it is time that we took a comprehensive view of this outer world which lies beyond the domain of sense.

What is the most striking difference between that world and this one? I answer, the world we are now living in is a material world, which to understand most thoroughly we must acquire a knowledge of the properties of matter. This we begin to do in earliest childhood by the use of our senses, and this we continue to do, to a greater or less extent, as long as we live, calling into play the reason, highest sense of all, as soon as it is developed; and by the use of this, the royal sense, with the others as its servitors, we may arrive at a very thorough comprehension of the world of matter, so far as its relation to our needs is concerned.

On the other hand, the world that lies before us is, above all else, an immaterial world, using the phrase to denote an almost entire absence of matter, but not in the least to indicate any absence of reality. No, for this future life is a reality more positive in its character than the foundations of the pyramids, and its manifestations, being neither more nor less than the manifestations of living beings, can only be understood when that fact is kept in mind. They do not lend themselves to the inspection of the curious, these denizens of another life, but when conditions favor, they take hold of human instrumentalities and wield them with a power and skill that defy all resistance for the time, and leave on all who are present an ineffaceable mark.

It may be objected that this statement is incapable of proof, that, of all who have crossed the line between life and death, none have returned to bring positive evidence of the existence of such an unknown country, inhabited in such a way. The contrary is asserted, and while facts do not need the bolster of argument, whoever is in possession of a fact can present arguments relating thereto tending to throw light upon it. It is asserted by those who claim to know, of whom the writer is one, that an inhabited domain is in immediate touch with the earth, although not discoverable by any of the scientific instruments of investigation, such as the telescope, the microscope, or the spectroscope, nor yet by the surgeon's scalpel.

The camera, however, which may be called an instrument of record, has, at certain times, produced evidence which has excited a vast amount of argument pro and con.

This will not now be entered into, but attention is called to a very important consideration bearing upon the whole subject.

CHAPTER IX.

I HOLD in my hand a lens. This lens, in its shape, resembles a certain other lens through which I look in examining it. It was, indeed, modeled after the other, which is a part of my organ of vision. I place the glass lens in a microscope, and a hitherto unknown world is revealed to me. It was there before, but I could not see it. Do I see it now *with the lens*? It is evident that the lens is merely an aid to vision, since the lens in my eye is also necessary to convey the picture to my mind.

But now another question: Do I see with the lens which is a part of my eye? Is not that also merely an aid to vision? Let us consider. Since I have two eyes, I may lose one of them without losing the power to see. If I am so unfortunate as to lose one, then, if the eye is not merely an aid to vision, but part of the vision itself, it would naturally follow that I should see only half as well as before; but this, very evidently, is not true.

I can read as well as ever. For the examination of anything on a flat surface, one eye is as good as two.

Notice, also, that the lens of the eye and the glass lens are not only alike in shape and transparency, but that both are composed of material substances that can be analyzed, and that both are used to acquire knowledge of such substances and the relations existing between them. The glass lens is merely a supplement to the lens of the eye. It is one step further removed from the vision, but even the lens of the eye itself is not the seeing power. That lies back of all.

Take now the ear-trumpet, a contrivance to concentrate sound to a given point. It is intended as an aid to hearing, but it is not inseparably associated with the power to hear. A person with normal senses does very well without it. How about the ear itself?

Does that constitute a part of the hearing power of a man? If it does, what is the necessity of the auditory nerve? If the hearing and the ear were one and the same, there would be no need of this connecting link with the brain. The external and the internal ear, like the ear-trumpet, are purely material, and by means of them we are able to cognize those material emanations called sound.

I speak of sound as a material emanation, because whatever sound comes to us through the ear comes from some material source. The ear, being material, is adapted to convey such emanations to the brain, through which the mind becomes conscious of their existence.

The sense of touch, also, is exclusively adapted to the acquainting of its owner with still another aspect of things material. Hardness, softness, smoothness, roughness, heat, cold, and other attributes of matter become known through this sense, and it may be considered a rule without exception that when the sense of touch is excited, some material object is responsible. The same thing is true of the senses of smell and taste, but as their field of action is comparatively limited, I will allow the first three named to represent the whole number.

The organs of sight, hearing, and touch, then, are the three principal avenues through which we obtain knowledge of matter, they themselves, however highly organized, being also material.

Now, I have said that there is an inhabited domain in immediate touch with the earth, although not discoverable by any of the scientific instruments of investigation. Sight, hearing, and touch do not sustain this, and declare such a domain non-existent. If we bear in mind that these organs deal with matter only, it may be freely admitted that they speak the truth. The world whose existence we are asserting is an immaterial world, and although it be immaterial, it can be shown that it has, nevertheless, a claim upon our profound attention.

Certainly, after what has been shown, it ought not to lose in interest on that account. *For, if our bodily senses are, by their very constitution, unable to bring us any reports save such as pertain to matter, their silence in regard to the world we speak of counts for nothing.*

But it may be said that all entities are material. This is a specious plea, but the generalization is too broad. Let us test it in a familiar way. Benjamin Franklin was one of the signers of the Declaration of Independence, and attached his name to the immortal document in a clear and legible manner. All this has to do with matter. Even the emotions which he may be supposed to have experienced while affixing his name, although not in themselves material, had a material effect upon his frame.

I say that those emotions were not in themselves material. I might take my stand here, but prefer to go one step further, and put a question: What were those emotions? and then add, This question is not in itself material.

It might be made a subject of thought. An essay might be written upon it, which would be esteemed good, bad, or indifferent, according as the author rightly apprehended the character of the man.

The question may never have been put into language before, but it is now a real entity, and our mental powers, acting freely, will have no trouble in so regarding it. It will be seen that, while it may become associated with things material, may be written so as to be seen, spoken so as to be heard, or even stamped to reach the apprehension of the blind, these material associations are no essential part of the question, since it might arise in the mind without any such aid, and be examined there without calling into play any one of the bodily senses, or any combination of them.

It may be said that this is an idle question, unworthy to take an important place in an argument, but it cannot be said that it is a foolish question; and it may well stand as a representative of other questions, questions which might have been substituted; questions which have arisen in many minds at the same time, and the answering of which has involved the overthrow of kingdoms, thereby demonstrating, if necessary, the reality of their existence.

CHAPTER X.

In order to make progress in the search for wisdom, it is necessary that we should bind ourselves to follow where truth may lead.

We cannot maintain our name as followers of the truth, if, whenever her footsteps turn in some particular direction, we refuse to follow, or if, whenever the path leads in the direction in which we have predetermined not to travel, we begin to cast aspersions on the sincerity of our leader.

All who would attain the freedom which large possessions give, must learn sometimes to lay aside prejudice of every kind, and follow according to the general law which bids us proceed until some real obstacle presents itself, or some real danger confronts us.

My illustration has led us to the point where it appears that we are able to say, Realities are not always material in their nature. In other words, materiality and reality are not inseparably associated. They may be separately considered, and dealt with as though not related. The question, What were Franklin's emotions when signing the Declaration of Independence? is a real question. In the world of mind it has a reason for existence, and because the world of mind is associated with the world of matter, and, in some ways at least, takes precedence, that which is real in its domain may be asserted as real in the presence and by use of some of the appliances of the latter.

The converse of the truth, that realities may be devoid of materiality, may be given here as an aid to the understanding.

Material things are not always *real* in their nature. The scenery of the stage, the portrait in oil, effigies in wax are familiar illustrations, and it will be observed that none of these are intended to deceive. They are merely examples of material things used in an unreal way.

In looking at them, we may, by the powers of mind which we possess, endow them with a temporary reality, which will aid in producing mental results, or we may refuse to so endow them, in which case they remain barren of effect upon us. I have given examples of things real but not material, and of things material but not real. Take another example of the first of these: The Society for the Prevention of Cruelty to Animals rests upon a basis that is not material. It rests upon an idea. If the idea that cruelty to animals is harmful, not only to them, but to those who inflict it upon them, could be at some future time disproved, then we should expect that the society would disappear. At present it is sufficient to say that the society has a *real* foundation which is in no danger of being destroyed.

CHAPTER XI.

IT will readily be seen that to take firmly the position that realities may be devoid of materiality involves a great deal, and those who endeavor to prevent this thought from taking root in any particular mind are apt to hold up before him examples of the immaterial which are not real. Most dreams are of this nature. Their confused outlines make temporary impressions on the memory and are then forgotten. But we have not to do with such as these. We recognize that real things may be material, such as certain houses, lands, or mountains, and that unreal things may be immaterial, like passing dreams just spoken of; but the immaterial which is none the less real is what we bring into view. And if we are ready to admit, or to go further and declare, that reality and materiality are not necessarily conjoined, we are then ready to give a fair hearing to the statement that a real but immaterial world, inhabited by real but immaterial beings, is in closest relations with our own.

These real but immaterial beings, because they *are* real and intelligent, are possessed of the primal attributes of all intelligent beings: they have memory, feeling, emotion, will.

In power they differ widely from each other, and in their essential character there are as many shades of difference as with mortals.

Let us speak first of their power. This is mostly exercised in their own field, that of the immaterial, yet to suppose that it is any the less real in its effects upon our lives is to forget how small a part our senses directly play in influencing our motives. The end and object of our efforts may be to obtain the means to gratify our senses or those of our friends, but the process through which we are obliged to work is so complicated, it involves the play of so many forces, it brings us into relations with so many people, each with his own plans and purposes, that we are continually making decisions based upon what we consider as probable, rather than certain, results. This is the opportunity of the spirits, and we often discover that all our efforts have simply tended to the advancement of others, while we are left in the lurch. The man who keeps his temper under such circumstances may be favored by the receipt of a thought-message. It enters his mind as ideas do, with a flash, and if he is wise he will carefully elaborate it into words. I have been working for myself only, bending everything as far as possible to my own enrichment. Others have been doing the same. What right have I to complain if they have done with me, by their superior power and foresight, what I have tried to do with them? None at all.

Morally we are on the same level. Let this misfortune be a lesson to me. Henceforth I will at least make an effort to do as I would be done by.

As he makes this resolution, a warm glow suddenly pervades his being. He feels at once lighter and stronger, and then perhaps he does a little thinking for himself. "If I believed in angels, I should say that they were near, and touched me then; I never felt anything like it." Little does he suspect the truth, that the whole idea which he so carefully elaborated in his mind had been flashed into it from without by an angel-friend, and that when it had borne its natural fruit in a good resolution, it became possible for the same friend to convey to him a touch of her own delight.

It may be objected that illustrations like these prove nothing as to the source of the experience; that to deny that invisible intelligences so play upon men is as rational, or more so, as to say they do. But we are not limited to such comparatively indefinite evidence. For nearly fifty years it has been permitted, or commanded, or both, that these invisible beings should demonstrate the reality of continued existence, and they have been doing so in a great variety of ways. For particulars, reference is made to the periodical literature devoted to the subject, and to the scores of books which have been written upon it.

It is not my purpose, however, to enter into this field of evidence with any approach to minutiæ, for it was not here that I acquired the ability to say, The occult world is a real, inhabited domain. I know whereof I speak.

CHAPTER XII.

In searching for truth in the fields of thought, we often run counter to our own prejudices, and almost unconsciously call a halt. There are some whose self-conceit is so great that they invariably do so the moment that any of their prejudices is in the slightest danger of a shock. But it is rather to the seeker who has in part divested himself from this hampering load, which he had perhaps inherited like a humor of the blood, that I now speak.

What is to be done? How proceed in such a case? The remedy is simple. Whenever you are dealing with abstract ideas, and find one that is refractory, either in itself for want of further analysis, or because of some special weakness of yours which incapacitates you from subduing it, never give it up; if you do, you will find yourself under it like a toad under a stone for an indefinite length of time. No, the right thing to do is to pass at once from the abstract to the concrete, and find in material things the counterpart of the truth under examination, and then proceed. The effect is often wonderful.

To illustrate. Suppose you are examining the abstract idea of the expediency of doing right. You may have some particular case in mind, probably will have, if the decision is to count for anything in your life. You may call to mind the famous saying, It is better to be right, than to be president. You will recognize the principle involved in this, but is it of universal application? you may inquire. Is there not some way by which I can take the free-and-easy course and yet incur no penalty? A great many people appear to be able to, why should not I? This is the point where you need to transfer the case from the abstract to the concrete form, and ask yourself, Suppose I were mixing chemicals according to a certain formula to produce a certain compound, and suppose one of the ingredients were wanting. Should I go ahead and trust to luck, and expect to get the compound just the same as though I followed the directions? Surely not. What would the science of chemistry amount to if such a thing were possible? How could anything new be discovered if the governing principles could not be depended on, or, in other words, if like causes did not *always* produce like effects, and unlike causes, unlike effects?

The most intrepid explorer in the scientific field might well despair of the prospect in such a case. But this is chemistry, and the laws of conduct are not so rigid, you may say. That is just where you miss the path. Until you attain to a belief in the unity pervading all things, from the lowest to the highest, this unity differing in outward appearance or manifestation only, and not in essential character, you will find no peace nor rest. The laws of conduct less rigid than the laws of chemistry? Say, rather, infinitely more so. For the higher the plane of action, the less likelihood is there of any superior force interposing to divert the current of events from its natural course; and the laws of conduct, remember, pertain to the life of the soul, which makes them higher than the laws of chemistry by two removes, for the laws of health relating to the physical body come in between.

But the laws of conduct are not well understood, you say. That, indeed, is true. We have only a few keys opening into this realm of the soul, and most people are content to take public opinion as a sufficient guide rather than to take the trouble to explore for themselves.

But it is the plane just below this, that of bodily life and death, which we are attempting more especially to elucidate. There seems to be no systematic teaching in regard to this that is worthy of the name of science.

The problem of life itself, what it is as a force differing from other forces, how to deduce from the manifestations of vitality what vitality is, remains unsolved. And why so? For a very simple reason. Because those who attempt the problem are unwilling or unable to conform to the conditions which they recognize as necessary in all other departments of scientific research. They do not study life *objectively*. They may think they do. They may think that to study life in other men or in animals is a truly objective method, but this is a fallacy.

The theory that life needs to be studied from an outside standpoint in order to be comprehended, is all right, but the man who uses his own life-force in studying that of other men or animals is not outside the subject of his thought at all. The active currents of his own being continually intervene to obscure the processes of thought and render his conclusions valueless.

It may be true that no other method which can be called objective is immediately apparent, but it does not follow that there is no other; and if we simply enlarge our ideas of what is possible, we shall find the true method to be just what we ought rationally to expect, and that is this: The student who wishes to solve this problem, either for his own satisfaction or for the enlightenment of others, must eliminate from the problem the one disturbing element, *his personal life-force*.

CHAPTER XIII.

Does it seem absurd to say that, in order to study life, a man must die? For that is what this method amounts to in the last analysis.

Now, I beg of you not to be unnecessarily alarmed. I have said nothing about burial. If death were only another name for annihilation, then death and burial would be inseparably associated, no doubt. But suppose it should be true that it is an error to associate the thought of annihilation with any man, is it not clear that whoever permits that error to have any place in his mind is sure to give a meaning to the word death which does not belong to it? Is it not evident that the thought of death in that case must borrow blackness and mystery of a kind that does not pertain to it? Most surely. But let it be said again, that death is a reality; it is not a fiction, nor a mere seeming. A man cannot possess bodily life and at the same time be dead. The two conditions are incompatible. Otherwise there would be no advantage to be gained toward the study of life by experiencing its opposite.

Shall I try to tell you, from the standpoint of experience, what death is? Perhaps it will be best to tell you first what it is not. It is not a snuffing-out like a candle, unless we could suppose one where the spark should remain quietly alive until the candle was relighted.

It is not a going to sleep, unless we assume it possible for the dream-life to be woven on to the daytime consciousness at both ends without a break, so that the dreamer, however strange may have been his dreams, and whatever the testimony of others may be, is able to say, with conscious truthfulness, I have not slept at all.

Death includes, without question, an entire suspension of bodily sensations and activities. The consciousness of *being*, however, remains, and with it, as a necessary consequence, the consciousness of being alive, however shut in by the enclosing walls of a senseless frame.

What is to follow does not occur to the mind. A peace that is absolute belongs to a death that is clean. Appetite of every kind is dead with the body. Desire is not; resignation takes its place. What is this resignation like? It includes a consciousness of a more potent yet kindly will, and contentment with the result of the action of that will.

The Giver has resumed His gift, the gift of life, for the benefit of him who has parted with it. The resulting peace is permeated with gratitude, not different in kind, although different in manifestation, from that which the little child expresses in every motion of his happy little body, when he seems to say continuously, I am glad to be alive. The man is glad to be dead.

Do you think it impossible that such an experience could come to any one who should afterwards recover life to describe it? Very likely. But stop for a moment and consider. When a man dies, the result may be said to manifest in a twofold way. First: To the man himself, who is, to say the the least, cut off from his customary outward activities. Second: To the world at large, where the word is passed around, Such a one is dead; and one acquaintance after another, as he hears the news, turns to a certain part of his mental organism and marks it down in black where it is not likely to be forgotten. Henceforth he will send out toward that friend, now become a name or memory, a different kind of mental current.

But wait: the word comes, Not dead after all—a false report. Immediately the operation is reversed. The black marks are rubbed out, the little switch is returned, and the friends all agree, to save troublesome thought, that the man who was supposed to be dead was not really so, and the old question asked by Job, If a man die, shall he live again? is prevented once more from obtruding itself.

CHAPTER XIV.

My aim is to make this book practical, that is, to clothe its thought in such garb as to render it available for use, not to scholars merely, but to all thoughtful minds.

I shall endeavor in this chapter to gather up a few missing links in my train of thought, and afterwards endeavor to give you a glimpse of the Beyond. The question I seem called upon to answer is, How can a man be alive and dead at the same time? and in order to answer it, it will be necessary to analyze the thought called death, and separate it into its various parts.

The man is dead, says local report, and the consciousness of society undergoes that natural change in regard to the man which I have described.

His name becomes associated with things that were, but no longer are. Even those who theoretically believe that the man continues to live either in happiness or misery, have, most of them, so little confidence in the theory which they have subscribed to, that they never dream of putting forth a mental current based on the theory. To all intents and purposes, society consigns the average man to annihilation, with a half-careless "Poor fellow, so he's gone. We'll see no more of him. Well, no time to weep, seeing as he didn't leave me anything. What new device for entrapping the elusive dollar shall I conjure up to-day?"

I am dead, says the man himself as the shadows which have been gathering upon his senses culminate in a rayless silence, and every thought of motion becomes a recollection, a mere theory of fancy, that will not even approach the dominion of the will.

Death, as a state of consciousness, is a thing entirely new to him, but he cannot reason on the subject. To reason is to live, to set the brain in motion, to perform mental operations; this is no longer possible.

What shall this state be compared to? It is like that of one isolated in a secret cell of his own house, the key turned on him from the outside, every avenue of communication cut off, dead to the world and all that it contains. If a total loss of appetite can be associated with the state, it might continue for an indefinite period; and if the power of thought-transference comes in, a new kind of life has been begun.

But science says that no man is really dead who still retains his consciousness, by which statement science belies its name. Calling itself knowledge, it spreads abroad its own ignorance. How many a post-mortem has been held in the hope of finding the secret chamber wherein that part of man which cannot die has gone to rest! How often the sweet peace of death has become a conscious madness, by this means, God only knows. Gentlemen, desist.

To find a chamber whose occupant is invisible debars you forever from obtaining the proof that you have found it. But perhaps it is not the soul itself that is the object of this search, but rather some special physical representative that might be found still quivering with life and so betray its master. All folly.

The soul when uncontaminated informs the whole outward body. It has its pains and illnesses, more or less affecting the outer form, yet all unrecognized in materia medica, and when its mortal brother is struck with death, bends all its energies to make escape, lest it, too, take on mortality. Failing in its effort to make a doorway for its exit, it suffers for awhile through sympathy, till the final moment sets it free from pain within its small dark house, no longer small, because made clear, transparent, by the touch of death, when the dying has been brave. No trace of foreign matter may remain to start a dissolution, in which case the soul preserves the body from decay without more trouble than a little watchful care.

Sight, hearing, touch, through vibratory currents reach round the world and even touch the clouds; the body has become, in fact, a mansion perfectly adapted to the needs of its proprietor, who finds a new world open to his delighted consciousness, and thanks God fervently for his perfect victory over death, as well as for his comfort and protection within the white, still walls which form, in fact, the first abiding-place of the spirit.

With this still form as passive aid, the soul, with little pain, is able to make the mental transition which its change of circumstance requires. No longer concerned directly with any thought based on material needs or material changes, it finds itself in touch with the moral causes which underlie these changes; and because moral force is most familiarly manifest in and through people, these, and their relations to itself, fill all the mental horizon.

In this new field of perception, nothing impresses more than the enormous differences in spiritual rank and attainment existing among mortals who, judged by tape-line and scale, stood fairly equal, and whom human law necessarily places on a plane of perfect equality, or perhaps, through its deference to wealth, makes unequal in the wrong way.

The thoroughness with which past illusions are stripped away from the mind tends to leave the spirit fairly aghast at its previous blindness.

Frequently forgetting that the motor nerves of the physical form are no longer responsive to its touch, it starts to rise, that it may go and tell the world of these wonders just discovered, but finds itself in the firm and quiet grasp of death, a touch that seems to speak and say:

"Never mind; that is all right. You forget you are not free. Lie still and learn your lesson."

"But shall I not return?"

"Possibly, but the mortal life is no concern of yours at present. You are dead."

All this as in a flash, for words do not belong to this state, ideas rather, the spiritual essences of thought that seem to need no time whatever to make their mark upon the mind.

To some of these the mind is so receptive that they sink at once to the very core of being, while others are held upon the surface.

This last communication, You are dead, is sure to be so held. It seems such an evident conclusion to respond, If I am dead, there is no death but this seems such a contradiction to life's long lesson, namely, that amidst a wilderness of uncertainties, death is the one thing certain. And then the recollection of the shrinking of the soul at thought of death, how to account for that, if there were no reality behind appearances so countless?

This in another flash of ideation that leaves a sense of mystery as of a problem not worked out, and which may not be while death as a condition rests upon the form. I say, may not be, but would not be understood to mean that the hindrance is mechanical in this case. A pure soul, even in death, has certain reserve forces which can be put in action if the need is great enough, but the consciousness of being in a friend's control, especially when that control is apparently absolute, will tend to check all restless impulse in this region of the dark, till now all unexplored.

CHAPTER XV.

But if the soul might not take up and solve the problem for want of time and space, we at this writing are not so limited.

First, let us state it clearly. If death does not mean a loss of consciousness necessarily, what is its distinguishing feature as compared with life? And what, if anything, is there in it to dread? The confusion of mind so general on these topics can be accounted for in a very simple manner.

The body has its life and its death, and the soul has its life and its death, and we have but two words to describe the four conditions. This makes it so nearly impossible to generalize on the subject and at the same time maintain clearness.

For while the student of natural history attributes life and death to the body alone, and the idealist goes to the other extreme and makes life and death purely subjective—attributes of mind, not matter—the philosopher who would have his mind open on both sides, not only to those thoughts which enter unheralded, but also to those which seem to have their origin in physical vibrations and enter the sensorium through the body,—the philosopher, I say, finds it necessary to discriminate carefully in the use of these words, life and death, and to make it clear which is meant, the body or the soul, whenever he attributes either condition to man.

I have said the two words cover four conditions. What are they? In the first the body is alive, and the soul is alive. Beautiful condition of ingenuous youth! In the second, the body is alive, and the soul dead. The man who by a course of persistent indulgence in all manner of crime and sensuality has stifled the voice of conscience, and finally reached the point where he is ready to say, "Evil, be thou my good," attains to a form of quiet.

The soul dies, and its decaying powers are absorbed by the body, which becomes henceforth an embodied poison, most dangerous and even deadly to the contact of the sensitive.

The third condition is that of the soul first described, in which the body has either temporarily or permanently parted with its life, while the soul remains intact. Still a part of the world's seething life, because action and reaction of the powerful causative soul-currents continue with such a soul, the interment of the body will decide whether the temporary physical death shall become permanent or not. In those exceptional cases where the body is preserved from the paroxysms of a blind grief which, when they include contact, tend to snap the last thread of vitality, or, still more important, from the embalmer's ignorant knife, which slays unnumbered thousands—when the body is preserved from both these dangers by a previous isolation, great possibilities are in store.

A forty-days' fast in the wilderness was the experience of one such soul, after which he was able to say of his bodily life, No man taketh it from me, but I lay it down of myself. I have power to lay it down, and I have power to take it again.

For his bodily life was restored to him, and death of the body had no more terrors to the man who had attained superhuman powers.

The fourth and last case, that where the death of the body follows that of the soul, will not be enlarged on.

There are such cases, but such can receive no lessons from a printed page. The language of events alone can reach them, and even when the soul is not dead, but rather entombed in the body, and rendered torpid for want of air to breathe, the effect is the same, so far as reaching them is concerned; the death of the body wakens such imprisoned spirits, only to plunge them into an untold agony of despair as they discover that life, with all its opportunities, has been worse than wasted, and a bare existence alone remains, minus friends, minus hope, minus resource of any kind even to conceal the abject poverty which is seen to be the direct result of wilful and persistent wrongdoing all the way to the bitter end.

If we can suppose that such a soul, at this twelfth hour, under the tremendous pressure of this awakening, should suddenly resolve to accept the situation, and to brace every nerve to endure the horrors of the event without complaint, while it would not be possible to say *when* there would be any change for the better for such a one, the reason would be because time is not to such a soul; while it still remains true that mercy is as truly an attribute of infinite power, as justice must always be.

If, on the other hand, we suppose that such a soul breaks out into rage at the discovery of its loss, hurling anathemas at the author of its being, it will thereby plunge itself into darker depths, parting with one after another of its faculties, until final extinction of the individuality closes the scene.

I have now shown the four conditions which our dual constitution in relation to life and death makes possible. Some enlarging on these topics, which concern us all, may not be unprofitable. We all enter life in the first described condition, with body and soul both alive, the body visible and tangible, the soul more or less so, according as its environments since conception have favored its growth.

Comparatively few of us ever reach the second condition I have described, in which the body remains alive while the soul is utterly dead. The protests of this, which is called the immortal part of us, because the death of the body in itself does not impair its vigor, usually prevent so great a calamity from occurring.

Some kind of a compromise is entered into, by which the soul is allowed a certain amount of freedom, on condition that the body shall remain undisturbed in its favorite pleasures. Sometimes one day in the week is selected, in which the soul is permitted to rule.

Sometimes a single department of life's activities is placed under its charge, and to meet the man on the favored day, or to have dealings with him in this favored department, gives you a very exalted idea of the individual. Sometimes in his business relations a man will be found conscientious in the extreme, while in his family he acts the tyrant and the brute. Sometimes his family almost worship him, while thousands speak his name with detestation. In either case the body, not the soul, the outer and visible, not the inner invisible self, is the leading factor in the man, and the court of last resort.

The man is still in slavery to the mortal; he has no knowledge of any life except the earth-life; the faith-knowledge which he might have, were his soul given its freedom and permitted to use its higher powers, is shut out by the disorder of his condition, wherein a servant in rank, the body, rules over the prince entitled to the throne.

This is the prevailing condition of the human family to-day, the difference between most people in this respect being merely one of degree, some giving the prince more, and some less of freedom. A few millions at most have given the nominal power into his hands, retaining the real for bodily uses. To curry favor with these, tens of millions profess to have done the same. In thousands only is the soul truly regnant, and these are widely scattered, and more or less hidden, lest they be driven out of life.

CHAPTER XVI.

WHEN I say that I have been outside and have returned, I speak the truth, and yet my words seem to express an untruth. It is because, as I have said before, that other kind of existence is so different from this that it uses a different language to express even a simple idea, a language which the kind we know as figurative most nearly resembles, although that is far enough from being the same. I should therefore use figurative language to embody what I have to say in regard to that other life, if literary considerations were alone to be regarded; but my aim is to benefit, and I decline to use a form of speech which has been so often sold as merchandise that many people no longer believe there is any truth attached to it. I use instead the plain, everyday speech, and say without qualification that I have been away, that I am acquainted with the conditions that follow after death, that I lean on no man's theories, not even on those which I might make, if I were given to theorizing, which I am not. No, I rest on facts, plain, cold facts, which are none the less so because they are registered in the mind of one man instead of many; facts of consciousness not to be gainsaid, although, in order to express them so as to make them most useful here, it is necessary to translate them into a language so far from the original, that only those who keep the fact of the translation in mind can hope to receive the truth in something like its purity.

I am well aware that I can scarcely hope to convince my reader that it could be possible under any circumstances for one to enter the kingdom of the dead, to take on the powers and conditions belonging to that realm, to become a component part of that world of mystery to the extent of dismissing all care in regard to the possibility of return, and even to transmit such a thought-message as this. The responsibility for my being out of place rests upon you all; I was compelled to undergo the pain of the passage at your will; and now that you repent and ask me to return, I will take my time and think about it. I am well housed in a good body on this side. I do not know that I would go back if I could.

That, after all this, and after a succession of spiritual events which, measured by their effect on one's consciousness, should correspond to a period of centuries on earth, one should actually make his way back and take up again the broken threads of his earthly life, and weave them into something resembling an orderly design once more, — to convince my readers of the possibility of this is so nearly impossible that I shall not seriously attempt it, although it is true.

It will be said that even though I suppose that this is actually true of myself, it does not follow that I am not suffering from an hallucination.

It will be argued very naturally that in so far as I am now a tangible, actual human being, just so far is it impossible that I should ever have been actually dead; and as to becoming habituated to the kind of life which may remain after the body loses its animation, for any one now living to make such a claim is the height of absurdity.

Any one who shall take this stand will need to be reminded that bodily consciousness is one thing, and soul-consciousness another, and that there may be *spiritual* existence beyond that. Comparatively few mortals have not at some time in their lives awakened at least momentarily to soul-consciousness, and can remember, if they care to try, how suddenly and completely the bodily consciousness retired into the background at its coming.

Thousands can testify that this soul-consciousness in them so dominates that of the body as to render bodily pains powerless to disturb the regnant soul.

These may be able to understand that in the world toward which they hasten, another advance will become possible, wherein the soul-consciousness shall become subordinate to the higher life of the spirit.

To make this a little clearer let me say that what you are now conscious of as your soul, the sensitive inner nature, that feels a slight as though it were a blow, that spurs the organism to years of anxious toil in the hope of gaining independence, that scorns to beg, yet in the hour of danger sometimes feels to pray—this inner self is to be your body when death shall come to break the tie that holds you captive in the dust. Every consideration to which your soul is now sensitive shall become, as it were, the laws of nature then. You will suddenly discover that ill-will, for instance, is a current actually tangible, as much so as an electric current was to your physical body. You will learn experimentally that kindliness of spirit, good-will, and gratitude are equally tangible to your new and finer senses. You will perceive that a generous spirit diffuses light, and a selfish one dwells in his own darkness, and this kind of light and darkness you will be astonished to discover has taken the place of what you formerly knew by those names. You will soon perceive that a deceiving spirit knows how to wear a false light as he pretends to a genuine interest in your welfare, and that a truly friendly one will sometimes hide his light, if thereby he can obtain advantage for your benefit.

If your life has been little more than a revolution around yourself, measuring everything by its relation to your personal advantage as you saw it, you will be surprised to find how small and dark a space will bound your being; and it may be a long time before you cease to dwell upon the memories of the world left behind, or cease to hope that in some way you can return to make a better use of its opportunities. And when you shall fairly come to understand that you have been living in the generous air and sunshine of the spirit of God, and that, instead of seeking to imitate Him by making your life a blessing to those less favored than yourself, you have employed your brief span in the effort to appropriate to your private use everything that could be lawfully seized on, you will wonder why the certainty that earth-life is limited had not impressed you more; and when you perceive, through the soul-consciousness which has taken the place of the bodily, that you have no data whatever upon which to base even a surmise as to how long your new kind of life is to continue, such measureless despair may fall upon you as shall even make tears impossible.

CHAPTER XVII.

ON the other hand, if anywhere along your life-journey you have scattered any seeds of kindness, they will every one of them bear fruit in the Beyond.

From the moment when you perceive and acknowledge to yourself that you are not in every way fitted to enter the courts of heaven and become associated with those to whom selfish thoughts have become simply memories, you are likely to have experiences tending to refine and purify your nature. No longer active in the outward, you must bear what influences come upon you from without as best you may. An infant in the cradle is not more helpless than the great majority of those who enter the Beyond; and the invisible nurse that may have you in charge will not ask you what kind of medicine is most agreeable, but will administer what is best for you.

Picture to your mind, if possible, what it would be like to lie physically helpless, with your outward consciousness telling you that you no longer appear as a man, or as a woman, but only as an infant to any eyes able to see you, while at the same time your mental vision is perfectly clear and takes in all your past life in every aspect of its relation to other lives, and especially in its relations to the great all-pervading life which seems now to be somehow lost out of all possible reach.

Suppose that while those reactions called pain and pleasure are more vitally potent than ever, because of a vastly heightened sensitiveness, mental as well as physical exertion has become impossible, a succession of states of consciousness taking their place; and then suppose a master hand, with all the resources of mesmerism at his command, should begin playing upon your organism, proving to you by every touch that not a line of all your past history but is an open book to him, and his only aim is to bring you to a willingness to confess your weaknesses and follies, your neglect of duties, as well as your open transgressions—one thing at least would surely result: you would discover, and never forget, that spiritual things are not less, but immensely *more* real than any physical entities with which you ever came in contact.

It is such a great mistake to suppose that because you have nothing in your experience corresponding to such a condition as that which I have just described, therefore you never will have.

What kind of reasoning can be weaker than this? Have you not two kinds of consciousness, one of the world and all it contains, and one of personal existence in its various relations? Do you not perceive that your body, vitally active as it is, and swayed by every thought you send out, belongs properly to the first of these fields of consciousness, while that which makes up your character—your preferences, your predilections, your faults, your foibles, your beliefs, and your prejudices—belongs to the second?

Can you not see that a suspension of the outward consciousness, in other words, a suspension of your power to sense the material world through your material senses, has no necessary connection with any suspension of your inner consciousness by which you might be able to say, I cannot move; I cannot see, hear, or feel anything, but I am still a white man, ready to swear by the flag and by my right to my personal liberty, and if any one takes the trouble to hunt me out he will find me the same man I always was?

Hundreds of thousands thus lie in their graves, thankful if they know its location, and waiting as only the dead can for the time of their deliverance.

CHAPTER XVIII.

Accept another glimpse of the Beyond. One of the most distinctive characteristics of this country or state of being is activity of mind. Let me explain why I say country or state of being. It is either the one or the other to the consciousness according to the point of view. Looked at externally, it is seen to be a new environment, a different kind of life; but when its atmosphere becomes yours, the effect upon your mental organism will be so great that you will rightly regard it as a state of being to which earth-life bears the relation of a pre-natal one. This comparison, however, has one defect, for while we of the earth have no conscious memory of our pre-natal life, they of the Beyond recall every leading event of earth-life as clearly as though no time had intervened.

The change of state brings on the mental activity spoken of, the effect of which on the material side manifests as heat or magnetism, or both.

The lifting off of the weight of dead matter causes a feeling of buoyancy, and the vibrations of the particles of the gaseous body may be so great that it will seem to expand until one seems everywhere present over a vast territory in the same way that we are now present in all parts of our physical bodies.

The first event of prime importance to you will be the demonstrating and establishing of your spiritual rank. Just where do you belong? In the society of what people, or what class of people, are you content? Does any accusation lie against you? If so, what have you to say in regard to it?

Are there any special credits that you claim which seem never to have been acknowledged? Is there anything you wish to confess? To what concealment do you claim a right?

The answering of these questions may be a very simple matter, or may involve the welfare of nations. While the friends left behind will contribute their quota of evidence, those with whom you have been associated who have preceded you to the unknown country will be the most actively interested in your case. You will find some waiting for your testimony on some point involving their own status, and when you come to speak of the matter you may have to struggle against a tumult of voices before you succeed in testifying. Where questions of fact are involved, of sufficient importance to justify it, most wonderful agencies can be set in motion to determine them correctly in the region of the Beyond.

That precise point in the ether where the event occurred, and which has long since been left behind by the passage of the solar system through space, can be visited and made to yield up its record as by kinetograph; or the surroundings may be reproduced as on a stage, and the one who persists in falsifying is suddenly placed there and told to act his part again according to his own story. He will find it very difficult to play a false part in the presence of those who know the truth.

It may be noted that this picture of a soul on trial is quite different from that given before, where it is held as the prisoner of death; but it is only necessary to bear in mind that events may succeed each other even in a country where time is not, and that such succession marks the stages of one's growth.

If any of your faculties are in a dull or torpid state because the circumstances of your life have been such that they never have been given a field of action, the invisible actors of the Beyond who may have you in charge will know how to awaken, stimulate, and call these faculties into an active state before the final decision is rendered, to the end that no injustice may be done you on their account. Should the verdict of the lower court be such that you are not willing to abide by it, you may take an appeal to a higher court.

At the last you may even appeal from the judgment of angels altogether, and demand a trial by the great Spirit of the universe, but you will not do this recklessly when you know that it involves a trial by ordeal, or a contest of sheer will-power, sustained by conscious innocence alone, with planetary forces.

Not brief nor trifling is a contest such as this; not once in a thousand years does such a thing occur; but the fact that the way to it is always open in the Beyond proves with what infinite tenderness the individual is guarded against injustice.

But it is impossible that I should know of what I am speaking, some reader says. I grant you that it seems so, but would discussion settle it? Is it not time the door was opened? Is there no need?

CHAPTER XIX.

An illustration of the difficulty of generalizing when speaking of matters on the spirit-side just now occurs to me.

Suppose that you as a mortal were permitted to witness a combat between a soul on its way upward and a foul spirit seeking to gain control. The spirit may be able to take on any form it pleases, and approaches in the guise of a friend. But the soul receives a warning touch and speaks out sharply: "Stand; keep your distance. Who are you? and what do you want?" With every smooth and crafty method of tone and word the spirit seeks to convince that he is what he claims to be, a friend, and entitled to approach. The soul, with its senses sharpened by fear, uses every effort to discern the character of the stranger, weighs and analyzes instantly every expression of the wily foe, and before the answer is completed, decides positively and prepares to strike. The spirit perceives the motion and shifts his footing in time to escape the blow—a thought-impulse, weighted to kill. Does the spirit respond in anger? Oh, no; his object is not to injure, but to gain control, so he remonstrates, with pretended grief, that one whom he loves should so mistake him. But the soul is not to be deceived, and gathers up its strength for another blow. The spirit pours out a perfect stream of flattering words, intended to lull his intended victim into a momentary lack of vigilance, and ventures a little nearer, hoping to touch the aura and disappear from view, only to become manifest as an invisible power within the soul, an active agent in undermining its powers until the opportunity shall present to seize the very throne itself and revel in the possessions of its victim.

But the soul is cautious, and in virtue strong, and so, conscious of invisible protection, suddenly fixes the demon with his eye, and before he can escape launches at him a bolt that leaves him helpless and writhing, dead as a spirit can be. "I killed him," says the exulting soul, as it passes on its way.

You would be apt to say, "He did not kill him at all; he only disabled him."

Now, while it is true that what I have described corresponds in appearance to what we should here call disablement merely, its full meaning cannot be understood without entering the consciousness of the spirit who was struck down.

To such a one activity, or the ability to act, constitutes life; inactivity, or the inability to act, constitutes death, not death as we know it, but a living death, in which the fierce vibrations of a life that knows no end, being confined as though by a broken wheel in its carriage,—being confined, I say, to the gaseous envelope, the propulsion of which has absorbed half its fire, soon heats the envelope to a torturing degree.

Illustrating in another way, the evil spirit, being disabled from continuing his customary activity, is forced to reflect, to look back over his course, and face the evils he has done. Horrors take hold of him. The most poignant dread of being overtaken by those whom he has despoiled of all that made life dear, until in despair they have committed suicide, and started out to find their tormentor, takes hold of the miserable wreck, who has not even the consolation of looking forward to some certain end to his sufferings, because neither time nor the last sleep are known in the region of the dead.

Is this experience, do you think, any less to be dreaded by a selfish spirit than is death by a mortal who is consciously not ready? It is therefore properly called death in the language of the spirit, made up, as that language is, of ideas only.

But in calling it death on the earth-plane we are using a word that has a much different meaning here.

When we say, "The man is dead," a funeral, or at least a burial is suggested. Not so there.

In this we have an example of the difficulty of conveying information in regard to the conditions of the Beyond, without using words that are liable to be misunderstood.

Only those who have attained to the ability to converse in the light, eye to eye, without words, are entirely free from these obstructions to mental intercourse.

CHAPTER XX.

ASTRONOMY teaches us that our earth, together with the other members of the solar system, is traveling through space, at the rate of eight miles per second, around a distant center, in an orbit requiring many thousands of years to complete.

We learn from this that we are constantly changing our place in the universe, and are entering new etherean fields, not only every year, but every day and hour. Since we are unconscious of this motion, it may seem to have no vital relation to us, yet, by a knowledge of the fact, we may gain an insight into the wonderful resources of this great machine for recording events.

Every thought and feeling of which we are conscious makes its mark, not only upon our bodies, both the outer and the inner, but also upon the ether through which we are passing. I am alluding not to the words in which we clothe or perhaps conceal our thoughts or feelings when communicating with one another, but to the thought-current itself at the point of origin.

This would be the same in the minds of all men of equal intelligence, without regard to nationality; and those beings who are able to read the marks left by these currents would find them written in unmistakable characters, and of a size proportionate to our rate of travel, on the fair ethereal page.

In one respect we are at an enormous disadvantage in our relations, conscious or unconscious, with the denizens of the Beyond.

Our thought-motions compared with theirs are like an ox-team to a locomotive. It is a fact, and there is no use in quarreling with it. On the other hand, through our association with matter we are able, without permanent injury, to bear oppressions of the spirit which would be death itself to them; and those among them who would take delight in insulting us are deterred from doing so by our insensibility to the stinging thought-current. We ourselves would not insult a post for being one.

These oppressions of spirit, or depressions, as we blindly call them, are a part of the system by and through which we are made to manifest what manner of person we are; and our blindness as to the real meaning of the life we have come into possession of, our persistent mistaking it for an end, instead of a means to an end, brings it to pass that the tests we undergo as to our fitness for this or that position in the real though hidden life that awaits us all, are real and genuine tests, which they could not be, to their full extent, if we clearly understood at the time just what was being done. Every thoughtful man and woman looking back over life can discern how this or that decision has been a turning-point leading on to unexpected success or paving the way to disaster or defeat. When the test is complete, some inkling of its meaning often dawns upon us, and we resolve to be on guard next time, and then perhaps we start off on some rainbow chase, only to discover that we are the prey of delusion once more. Then, perhaps, we get angry and curse the whole machine as the product of some stupid blunderer, thereby avoiding the confession of any mental obliquity on our own part.

Not all of the delusions of mortality are of a kind that lead to such a result. Some have been imposed upon us by our risen brothers of the other sphere, and have held sway over our minds, as they did over our fathers' minds, and over their fathers' before them, none of us living long enough on the mortal side, or obtaining sufficiently clear independent light, to enable us to become free. The shaking off of the fetters of this mental bondage is a special characteristic of our own day; and those who have listened to the torrents of eloquence poured from the lips of the young mediums upon this subject, know that this work, the necessity for which, as I have indicated, is largely due to other-world intelligences, is now being forwarded from the same quarter with tremendous power. Verily, there must have been a revolution in the heavens, or this would not be. And such, indeed, is the case. The tremendous power of an organized hierarchy under the controlling influence of a single mind so prominently in evidence here, is without a counterpart on the other side to-day, although the sins against humanity which have been charged against the priesthood of past ages should more properly be laid at the door of their invisible inspirers, then in the height of that power which is no longer theirs. To-day the enemies of racial progress are to be sought for on earth, where the intoxicating dreams of power without responsibility have found lodgment and worked their corrupting influence in the minds of not a few of our brothers, who seem to forget that they are still members of the race they are seeking to enslave, and that their responsibility for misusing the power entrusted to them will be accounted all the greater in consequence.

CHAPTER XXI.

The range of subjects coming within the scope of my title is so great that I cannot undertake an exhaustive treatment of any within reasonable limits, but I hope to supply a few keys by the use of which reverent minds of any and every school of thought may be able to enter upon successful explorations.

The amount of evidence necessary to convince a sincere inquirer that this earth-life, important as it is, is but the threshold of existence, is not very great, but it must needs be adapted to the individual mind.

To obtain this evidence is worth more to any man or woman than any other purely mental acquirement can be.

For it is a mental acquisition, the possession of which is related to, and has a natural influence over, every other we can call our own. Yet it has not, in itself, any transforming effect upon the life and character.

When such a result follows, other influences share in the work. He who has lost friends that were a part of his life, the mother whose children have fainted away into the world of mystery, the philosopher who has given the strength of his years to the search for truth, are all profoundly affected by the discovery; while those in whom the affections are less strongly developed, or whose mental powers give them no adequate perception of the profound and far-reaching relations of this great truth, may hold it as lightly as they do their dreams, and receive from it no more benefit than they do from them.

Whoever is capable of analyzing a thought or the expression of a thought, can find evidence of the world beyond strewn along his path on every hand.

All figurative expressions are merely unconscious devices to give to thought somewhat of the objective reality it possesses to dwellers in the Beyond. For instance:

"There are names which carry with them something of a charm. We have but to say 'Athens,' and all the great deeds of antiquity break upon our hearts like a sudden gleam of sunshine; 'Florence,' and the magnificence and passionate agitation of Italy's prime send forth their fragrance towards us like blossom-laden boughs, from whose dusky shadows we catch whispers of the beautiful tongue."

Is it doubted that the Athens of which the author speaks will be found embodied in forms real and tangible in that other world which takes to itself all that attains to immortality in this one?

Why do authors speak of a *cold* greeting, of *walls* of reserve, *rivers* of kindness, or the *sunshine* of love?

They may not be able fully to explain, but expressions like these point to features of the landscape in that world where the inner becomes the outer and takes on those garments of reality which belong to it by right.

The things which are seen are temporal, but the things which are unseen are eternal, and when we have broken connection with our temporal bodies, or attained a true and perfect control over them, we may enter into this knowledge, to find it truly a heavenly inheritance.

But it is not alone through figurative and poetic language that we may discover evidence of the existence of an immaterial world.

The broad fields of philosophy and literary criticism receive their light, their water, and their air, outside the world of sense almost entirely. Scarce anything in these domains has any causative relation with the world of matter.

For instance, take this passage from one of the magazines:

"But what does the work of higher criticism really mean? It means, briefly, as applied to the Old Testament, the revision of certain traditions concerning the structure, the date, the authorship of the books—traditions which had their origin in the fanciful and uncritical circles of Judaism just before, or soon after, the Christian era."[2]

A careful analysis of the meaning of this will show that it begins and ends in the domain of abstract thought. To use a figurative expression, it does not touch the ground anywhere. If our bodies and their needs, if the earth and its products which minister to those needs, if, in brief, the material universe really comprised the *all that is*, such a thought as is contained in the passage quoted could never have come into being. For it has no practical relation to things as such.

Yet there is nothing especially obscure about it. It was written for men and women of ordinary intelligence, who are supposed to take an interest not merely in sacred truths, which, indeed, are not dealt with in the article from which I quote, but the structural forms containing those truths.

All of which, rightly interpreted, points to another phase of existence, which is either near to or far from us according to the stage of our development, a phase which may become measurably real to us even before we enter fully upon it, and which has the strongest possible claims upon our attention.

---

[2] *The Arena,* January, 1894, "The Higher Criticism."

CHAPTER XXII.

THERE is no more fruitful source of error to the student of occult philosophy than the assumption which he continually makes, that the race and the individual may be treated as one when their relations to a higher power are being considered.

It appears that the study of the laws of chemistry may be partly responsible for this. A molecule of any substance, having in itself all the properties of that substance, may be reasoned upon and regarded as though it were, as it is, an epitome of the mass. In the same way it is assumed that man, the individual, is an epitome of the race, and that, in endeavoring to obtain a philosophical view of him, we may pass in review before the mind what we know of the race, and what we know of the individual in a general way, without drawing any line of distinction between what is true of the one and what is true of the other.

Now, while this mental process may have a certain value when both are considered externally, those who attempt to solve the deeper problems of the race or the man, by means of it, are sure to fall into error.

It is not borne in mind that our race is scarcely conscious of itself as a unit, and if it were, it would in the present state of knowledge regard itself as alone in the universe, flying through space on a revolving globe with enormous velocity, along an unknown orbit. There may be other inhabited worlds peopled by other races of beings, but as a race we do not know this to be true; and only a dim perception of the survival of a few of its own members that have lived their little lives and passed away since time began, relieves the sense of isolation with which the race looks out into the surrounding darkness.

The student of history contemplates the rise and fall of nations and traces the causes which have led to their overthrow. He observes the same influences at work to-day as in the olden time, and when the premonition of like disasters comes home to him, he is ready to exclaim, "There is no hope! There is no God!" And in so speaking he gives utterance to the soul of our race, which is still groping in the darkness for light and a place of rest.

How much of this is true of man as an individual? Very little, comparatively, as we shall see. In the first place, as individuals, we are conscious of companionship. We look around us and out over the world and see great numbers of our fellows whose life and surroundings are comparable with our own. Such differences as we perceive in each other only give evidence that our fellow-beings are real, not simply reflections of ourselves; are objective entities, not elusive shadows. And by as much as we are conscious of an individuality apart from that of our race, by so much may we hope to separate the thread of our destiny from the tangled mass.

Examples of such a separation are to be found among the great names of the earth; and a study of their lives will teach us how best to shape our own. It will also teach us that race-life and individual life are not necessarily the same, that the individual may absorb light for which the race is not yet ready, and set his standards of thought and action far beyond what is yet possible to the race as a whole.

If, now, we form our conceptions of the character of the power overruling us, by an exclusive study of those events which affect great numbers, we are liable to serious error. If the sound of thunders intended for the ear of the race be concentrated so as to fall upon our individual hearing, they will certainly deafen us completely.

On the other hand, those whose narrower vision sees only the play of events as they affect the lives of individuals are also liable to error in forming their estimate of the character of the overruling power.

Here tragedy visible and invisible plays its part, and sometimes injustice in the extreme appears to triumph. There is no possibility of avoiding error in judgment from this point of view, without constantly bearing in mind at least three things: first, that outward disaster is sometimes an inevitable result of long-hidden crime; second, that to the innocent, death is a release from prison, a promotion from a lower to a higher sphere of action, and that those who are able to look beyond the instruments used to break their fetters, to the kindness that sets them free, can mount on the wings of delight to a diviner air; and third, that the dwarfing of the faculties of a soul during the short space of earth-life will turn out to be a far less serious matter to the soul than to the one responsible for it.

CHAPTER XXIII.

THE question may be asked, Wherein lies the difference between man the unit, and the race which is an aggregation of these units? What philosophical difference is possible? In answer, I would say that while the individual and the race alike possess body and soul, the individual at times manifests a power of becoming greater in every respect than the influence of heredity or surroundings can at all account for. Such individuals tell us of some powerful influence descending upon them, as it were, from a higher sphere, and to this they attribute the changes in their life and powers which make all their friends to marvel. No such stimulating and transforming influence has ever manifested itself on so broad a scale as to affect our entire race at once, and we must conclude that the time has not come for such an event. As a race, our eyes are not lifted above the earth. We care little about our origin, and still less about our destiny. The love of war and bloodshed, delight in the flowing bowl and all its attendant revelry, are still characteristic of our race, and the heavy clouds that are gathering in our sky are not yet black enough with impending evil to arrest us in our downward course.

Ah! well for us it is that we are not to be left alone to rush headlong to destruction in our blind folly. Terrible as are the forces we have invoked against ourselves, those which shall save us from death by all manner of intoxication are infinitely greater.

The wasting fever of war undoubtedly must come, such war as the world has never seen before, but when the coveted excitement, changed to agony untold, is at last over, when our physical forces are entirely exhausted, the loving Parent whose outstretched hand we have always refused, will show a pitying face. A draught of infinite peace will be imparted to our spirit, and we shall rise in newness of life to enjoy the forgotten delights of obedient childhood, and make this old world over into one entirely new.

CHAPTER XXIV.

I HAD not thought to touch this strain when I began to write of the Beyond, but some things almost write themselves, and I have not forgotten the closing words of the appeal with which this book opens. "We are trodden down by our brothers among the living. Help us, our fathers from the dead."

Ah! if the wire which carries this petition outward can bear the strength of the return current, it may possibly convey such tidings as words are not able to express, for is it not true that the sweetest strains are cradled within a silence which speaks more profoundly to the soul than does the music to the ear? Let us hearken.

"Do you wish to know what stands in the way of our coming to the rescue? Nothing but your unbelief in the possibility of our coming. Thank God that unbelief is growing weak. Could you know what exhausting labor is ours in our efforts to reach you, you would pray rather for light to enable you to do your part. Believe, oh, believe that we have not forgotten. In agony of spirit we are striving to awaken you from slumber, to instil into your minds the supreme truth, that no good thing that can be named is impossible of occurrence. You are ready to believe it for the material, why not accept it in the spiritual?

"Religious liberty is your priceless privilege. Can you possibly gain it by setting foot on religion itself? Be sane. Learn to discriminate. Throw away the chaff, but keep the wheat. Death is a magician, not a murderer. The pain all comes beforehand. The passage itself is not painful. Death merely turns the key in a door you never saw before, and you step out into such a freedom as you never dreamed of. 'Be thou faithful unto death, and I will give thee a crown of life,' suggests a great truth. Try to get hold of it. No man, and no body of men, no spirit, nor any combination of them, can prevent you from making your life a success. There are prizes to be won. Why not try for them?

"But you say you are trying. Sword in hand, you are battling for the right. Yes, we know, and sometimes you are wounded, and help seems never to come. Hold fast. We are building a road.

"It is already finished, and the cars are on the track. You shall not die of wounds like these. Help is near. Your prayer is heard. We knew it would be. From the heights beyond the heights has come the order, 'Descend in power. Earth's children are ready to receive you.' And we are not few nor weak. Our phalanx moves in a light which nothing can withstand. Believe it, and stand upon your feet. We are already here."

CHAPTER XXV.

THERE is another grand division of my subject, but the difficulty of presenting it through the medium of written language is even greater than that already dealt with, and only a slight attempt will now be made. Not only do thoughts take the place of timings in the Beyond, but *emotions take the place of forces*. By emotions in this connection I mean those currents of energy which have their rise in, and are more or less under the control of individualized intelligence, as love and hate, joy and sorrow, hope and fear, happiness and distress; and by forces I mean those which are sometimes called blind forces, such as attraction in its various forms, heat, electric vibration, and the like. As these last pertain especially to matter, we should expect them to retire into the background in a world where mind-realities, or facts of consciousness, absolutely dominate. And so they do. And here may be a good place to indicate what part matter really plays in this immaterial world. Let me call attention to the world of art. Let us recall its great names, and the masterpieces which have given them fame, the wonderful poems, the paintings, the sculpture, and the musical creations that will never die, and then pause and consider how slight are the demands made by this wonder-world on the lower world of matter. The poet and the musician call for writing materials, the sculptor needs some clay and a few modeling tools, the painter some pigments and brushes, and a bit of canvas. With these slight aids the noble conceptions of genius are materialized for the delight of future generations.

Take another illustration. When a ship goes out of the harbor, it is to be assumed that she takes her anchor with her, and carefully guards it against possible loss.

It is likewise true that within the scope of the great and splendid activities of a free spirit, a material anchor is somewhere safely cared for, yet such an anchor has no more prominent relation to the activities of the spirit than the anchor of a ship has to the ship's power to cross the sea. If we could think of a ship with nothing else to do but to lie around the harbor, the relative importance of the anchor would increase very much; and if it had no anchor of its own, it might attempt to tie up to some other vessel that had one. And so with earth-bound spirits whose testimony is sometimes quoted to the effect that spirit-life is as dependent on matter as any other. Most of them are blissfully ignorant of their own poverty, and move about the earth, that is to say in the lower or earthly strata of thoughts and feelings, because they have no desires above them.

They remember this life as a lost heaven, and are continually bemoaning that loss in secret, while their activities take the form of influencing mortals to this or that kind of sensual indulgence, which they wish to share through sympathy. Every impulse and desire is bent upon a possible recovery of the earth-life, and they are so ignorant of, and indifferent to, any higher form of life, that it remains without existence to them.

I would not say they are insensible to the enlargement of their powers consequent upon their release from the confinement of an earthly body. They could not be. Their discovery that death does not destroy the inner consciousness was a great surprise to them, but the novelty of the discovery soon wore away. What seemed so strange at first, became a truism, a simple scientific fact, previously unknown, and unable in itself to supply any stimulus to their higher powers.

It is evident that the testimony of these upon the subject is worthless, while those who have battled for and won the prize of recognition in a higher sphere give abundant evidence of their freedom from the bondage of matter, and the desires that have material things for their object.

Resuming my subject, not only matter, but those forces which are inseparably associated with it, retire into the background, nay, almost disappear, in the Beyond. Emotions take their place.

The atmosphere, or that which corresponds to what we know by the term, seems charged with some powerful element, resembling electricity in its effects, but differing from it in that it seems to be sensitive to thought, and to be capable of responding to it with dynamic force. A shock from this element is in every respect as real to the consciousness as an electric shock is to us. It comes from without and expends its force upon the gaseous body. Being sensitive to thought, it does not impress one as being capricious in its nature, but as though acting according to some law which it is of the highest importance to discover, if possible.

With the perceptive and intuitional faculties wrought up to the highest state of activity, it is presently discovered that it is not thought in the abstract, but thought surcharged with feeling or with devotion to a principle, some cherished sentiment of the soul, which has the power to excite this hitherto unknown element; and gradually it dawns on the mind that this element corresponds to public opinion on earth, that it emanates from the inhabitants of that part of the spirit-realm, and that if your mind does not happen to be in accord with theirs, you must either get away or do battle for your life. By life, I mean your power and freedom of expression, the very breath of the spirit, what a printing-press is to a newspaper, cut off from which, the paper is dead.

Manifestations of emotion, both in kind and degree, depend upon two things, our spiritual state or condition, and the nature of our surroundings. Passing over the first of these, it is evident that earth-surroundings greatly limit the expression of emotion; and when we observe the effect of a powerful current of this kind upon the physical tissues of the body, weakening and consuming them as by a flame, we see that the length of our stay here is involved in our ability to control our emotions.

Not so in the Beyond, where our stay is without assignable limits, and where the pent-up emotions of a lifetime at last find vent, and pour themselves out as by flood-gates to the sea.

And it is here that music plays its part in that wonder-world. For as ideas have each their appropriate form, so every emotion has a musical strain peculiar to it.

And who can describe the healing power of music under a master's hand? Reading the mind and soul as an open book, and informing every tone with the vibrations of a perfect sympathy born of knowledge, he administers to the soul whose life has been a tragedy long-drawn-out, such throbbing waves of strength and consolation, himself remaining hidden, as seem to issue from the very stars, and drown the memory of that age-long pain in an ocean of oblivion.

Ah! believe me, it is another world, where the powers of this one do not rule.

CHAPTER XXVI.

AND yet, as I have indicated, it is possible to live so far below one's moral and spiritual possibilities, that the loss of life will seem the loss of heaven, and the men of power on earth whom one has envied will come to seem very gods, worthy of being worshipped. Such a delusion as this is in part due to the absence of a common time-element.

Duration is measured only by the succession of various states of consciousness, and these change so rapidly under the influence of the vibratory intensity of the new life, that the events of a day lengthen it out until it seems like a year upon earth; and day and night being one in the Beyond, so far as activity is concerned, although they differ somewhat in magnetic conditions, when one of these year-long days is past, the spirit, glancing across into earth-life, at some money king, with thirty years of active life before him, can scarcely avoid endowing him with a kind of immortality, and may devote the fiery energies of the soul to building up the fortunes of such a one, with no higher object than that of keeping the mental balance and avoiding reflection.

This necessity for keeping the balance supplies motive for a great deal that is done by spirits in the lower strata of life in the Beyond. It is not, strictly speaking, mental balance, but organic, affecting the whole being. A spirit possessed of any conscious individuality whatever must generate a certain interior force to maintain it. This keeps his body in a state of equilibrium between the inner and outer pressure, and the body of a spirit is naturally as valuable to him as ours is to us. It protects him against currents of thought and emotion that are not adapted to his needs, and when evenly balanced he is able to put forth effective will-power along the plane of his development and below.

Any one who has not learned what soul-action is will have it to learn soon after the exchange of worlds. No other form of activity is possible there. No spirit strikes another with his hand, nor presents him with a visible token of wealth, yet battles are fought and presents given. As a suggestion: when you say to your friend, "Good-bye and good-luck to you," you are making him a spiritual present, although you may not be aware of it.

Whenever you launch a curse, if only in thought, you strike a blow, against which conscious rectitude is an actual armor, and the only one.

The very slightest impulse of ill-will directed toward any one is an action of the soul that may do real harm, and certainly makes a record.

These statements will commend themselves as true to most of my readers, many of whom, however, would not be able to explain why they are so sure of what they have learned from no teacher, and cannot recall from the pages of experience. Let me suggest.

From six to nine hours' sleep is an essential part of our daily lives. We suppose ourselves to actually sleep, not only in body but in mind and soul as well. Perhaps some who have very little mind and even less spirit, do sleep when their body sleeps, but there are very large numbers of people who, the moment the brain becomes quiescent, enter at once on the most active part of their daily existence.

This is especially true of such as during their waking hours have attained some knowledge of spiritual values, and have taken their stand on this or that platform of principles, religious, moral, or even political, and who would be ready to contend in argument, or even, if necessary, take up arms, in defense of their positions; in other words, who have a conscious location in some field of thought or fortress of belief.

The extent to which we influence others, or are influenced by them, during our sleeping hours, very few realize, because unable to recall, when waking, the experiences of the night just passed; but be sure that no reform can ever make much progress until the agitation for it becomes sufficiently powerful to link the day to the night, and engage the activities of partially freed spirits while their bodily consciousness is lost in slumber.

It is here that lessons are learned and impressions made, the recalling of the results of which may surprise us as to the extent, and puzzle us as to the origin, of our knowledge.

Readers of Emerson will find this a key to some of his mysterious yet delightful sayings.

CHAPTER XXVII.

Those who have never entered into any kind of associate life where they might learn to think and act for others as well as for themselves, will have a particularly hard time on the other side.

For no one can go through life without becoming responsible for innumerable acts, even if he does nothing more than make room for himself, and defend his own footing; and if he persists in living for himself, it follows that his motives will never rise above the care of himself, and, possibly, of those who contribute to his comfort.

If such a man, by speculation or otherwise, becomes able to surround himself with the tokens of wealth, there will not be wanting those who will bow low to him; and when he is called out of life, with perhaps no particularly heavy weight on his conscience, he will strut into another world carrying with him a very large sense of his own importance.

Now, there is no need to enlarge upon the emotions he will arouse, the intense though secret hilarity with which he will be taken in hand, and the endless variety of hazing operations to which he will be subjected; but he will be sure to make the unexpected discovery that death is a lost friend, long before the last spark of self-conceit is extinguished within him.

It is scarcely possible to convey an idea of how small a part individual egotism is allowed to play in the world beyond.

In this world our race, as a race, is under protection. We are all more or less conscious of this in our own person.

Even the most stolid, when suddenly reduced to the extremity of distress, find themselves calling upon God, almost without conscious volition.

If it were not so, if this protection were withdrawn, our race would shortly cease to be.

In the spirit-world, or in that part of it which adjoins this, figuratively speaking, which we enter as individuals, this sense of a general protection disappears. We find we are to stand or fall on our own individual record. We cannot lose ourselves in the mass. There is no mass. Time and space no longer exist for us. They are gone with the bodily senses and mathematical reasoning to which they were a prime necessity.

Sight, hearing, and touch of the soul have awakened, however, and how to use these new senses whose field of action is so immensely greater than the senses we have parted with, engages our attention.

Their first reports are so different from anything we have known that we discredit them entirely, are sure we must be dreaming, and put forth strong efforts to wake up. Failing in this, we look about us and endeavor to get our bearings.

Although time and space have left us, eternity and infinity have taken their place, and a feeling of awe steals over us at the realization, a feeling that extends in part to ourselves as we discover a certain element within us which now for the first time recognizes its home.

Then, in a flash, we perceive as never before, the essential narrowness of the limits of earth-life, and our mental vision shows us that whatever may have raised that phase of existence above the merely sensual or animal, had its home in the Beyond, and was only a visitor on earth.

We find ourselves ushered into the domain of causes, and a thousand perplexities of memory disappear in a magical way, as we become sensible of the tremendous force of the activities at work in this heretofore hidden realm.

A spirit sometimes finds himself as if on a stage, and the pressure of a powerful will bids him to act out his own character. He consents, for why should he not? Scene follows scene; men and women from every walk of life, those whom he has known, and those of whom he has read, appear and act their part; kings and courtiers come and go, prophets and peasants, soldiers and merchants; and he finds some link connecting him with them all. Perhaps a plot is formed to destroy his reputation; thread by thread the web is wound about him. How shall he get free? Is it not all a dream? But he is made to feel that he must not insist upon knowing. Something like an electric shock answers his thought, and bids him to consider his surroundings real, whether they are or not, and forbids him to think of such a thing as applying a test. And, indeed, there is small leisure for anything of that kind. He finds himself obliged to put forth energies he never dreamed of possessing, to keep from going distracted. The stage widens until it becomes the floor of a world. The audience swells to millions. He reaches out for their sympathy, but they do not respond. They do not pretend to know whether he is a true man or a scoundrel. If he cries, "I am true," they answer, "Prove it." What can I do to prove it? But they turn away unconcerned, while another strand of falsehood is thrown around him and he is brought to his knees, where he is made the target for scorn and contempt, which come like arrows to pierce his form. In the depth of his despair, he sends out a piercing cry to the spheres above him for help.

Just then he discovers that he is clothed in armor, with a good sword at his side. He did not know it before, he could not possibly say how or whence it came, but it is not a time for curious questions. He seizes the blade and with one sweep severs the cords that bound him, stands upon his feet, and then, in a voice that startles himself, he calls upon his enemies to show themselves. Instead of that he hears their retreating feet, the clouds lift, the applause of the audience gives him back his lost strength, and he is ready for the next ordeal.

Now it may not be supposed that during such a scene as this, it would be possible for the spirit to receive and answer thought-messages from his friends on earth, but it is even so. A spirit with a heart will at least make the effort to respond to every demand made upon it, but if among the circle of his friends one sends out the message, "Come now, if you care anything about me, I wish you would help me find this gold-mine. What do you have to do anyhow?" the spirit may be excused if he fails to respond, and does not immediately proceed to explain just what he has to do.

THE END.

Lector House believes that a society develops through a two-fold approach of continuous learning and adaptation, which is derived from the study of classic literary works spread across the historic timeline of literature records. Therefore, we aim at reviving, repairing and redeveloping all those inaccessible or damaged but historically as well as culturally important literature across subjects so that the future generations may have an opportunity to study and learn from past works to embark upon a journey of creating a better future.

This book is a result of an effort made by Lector House towards making a contribution to the preservation and repair of original ancient works which might hold historical significance to the approach of continuous learning across subjects.

HAPPY READING & LEARNING!

LECTOR HOUSE LLP
E-MAIL: lectorpublishing@gmail.com